THE GREY MOUND AND OTHER POEMS:

A Bouquet of Thoughts and Sentiments

Mathew Joseph

MJ Publishers

CONTENTS

Preface

The idea of bringing out a collection of my poems came to me only after my retirement. My working years had kept me far too busy to entertain any such thought. But when I went about searching for my poems, which I thought existed somewhere, I made the discovery that most of them had done the vanishing trick. As it was too late by then to turn back from my project, I decided to fill the gap by writing new poems. So, with the exception of six or seven pieces, all the poems in this volume are recent compositions. This experience convinced me that necessity can be the mother of poetry as well.

A subject-wise classification of these fifty poems will reveal that a half of all the poems here are Nature poems or very close to being Nature poems. The remaining poems include thumb-nail sketches of interesting individuals, childhood memories, records of significant experiences or situations, reflections on various matters, tributes to individuals or institutions, poems on the human destiny and so on. There are poems of explicit statement as well as poems where what is stated happens to be just the fringe of what is not said. As for the formal aspect, there are both metrical and free verse poems although these poems are by and large conventional. The metrical pieces include stanzaic and blank verse poems, lyrics, monologues, sonnets, sestinas and so on. I have not taken too much freedom with the form of my poems because it is my conviction that it cannot be distanced with any more than the conventions of a game.

Whether a poem will strike a responsive chord in the

heart of the reader or whether it will make him turn away from it in disgust depends primarily on what the poem has got to say. The second consideration is the manner in which the poem communicates its message. A third factor—it is not directly related to the poem—is the reader's susceptibility to poetry. No two readers are alike: If there are readers who will hear poetry even in the song of a bird, there are also readers who consider poetry largely unnecessary—people like the philologist brother of G.M. Hopkins who defined poetry as the poorest way of putting things. I have already commented on the first two of these factors and I am not overmuch bothered about what reception these poems will find at the hands of the readers. Poetry is its own excuse for being, but I will be extremely happy if anyone discovers in these poems even a faint glimmer of the 'fine frenzy' Shakespeare attributes to poets. I do not hazard any opinion on my own poetry because I hear in my imagination the reader say:—"Judgement is mine."

My idea of poetry is the old description of it as a very special way of using the language with the intention of exciting pleasure with the help of beautiful, elevated and imaginatively transformed thoughts. What I look for in a poem is the glow of imagination which has the power to transform thoughts much in the same manner as fire transforms a dull-looking piece of iron into brilliant incandescence. Whether my own poems are possessed of this glow—that is for the readers to judge. I will be happy if the readers acknowledge them as poetry or at least do not blame me for not having presented these thoughts in prose.

Dr.Mathew Joseph

1.THE GREY MOUND

There lay a mound of ashes in a field,
A cartload of greyness from a pit nearby,
Waiting for the rains to loosen the ground
So might the ploughshare help it drape the earth.

A bird alighted on the mound and scratched
Its barren deadness, hoping to unearth
A grub or worm, which it would ne'er find there,
Or would it? Why! The burnt out pile of ash,
I should have thought, was life's pile, a phoenix
Waiting for rebirth in life's myriad forms.

I knew the green stuff that the ash-pit burnt.
Those are now ashes that were once the proud
Branches of spreading trees which the farmer
Sacrificed, though with an unwilling heart,
So that the sun be pleased to kiss his crops.

The greyish grains are going back to the trees
Or to what ports of life will receive them.
The grey will grow green or yellow or red
And smile with the flowers or dance with the leaves.
They'll plump the fruits or swell the gourds or grain
The hardy wood, or by Nature's magic changed,
Transform as nectar in a floral bell.

The bird flew up with something in its beak.

MATHEW JOSEPH

Think this of the mound, if you find it gone
When you come again: The phoenix has risen
From its ashes and is on the wing again.

2.THE ISLAND AND THE LAGOON

An isle it was of brownish sand,
A sterile patch of modest size;
A wayward child of the mainland
That had strayed off, for so it seemed.

A mile out in the blue lagoon--
  Itself the sea's wild, errant child--
The barren islet lay at noon
  Bereft of all that isles boast of.

A bird or two, some driftwood, crabs,
  Puddles, boulders, soggy ground:
The sea it grabbed in drifts and drabs;
There was no poorer isle around.

What is an island if no plants
In graceful green clothes drape it bright?
What's an island where the wind chants
The praise of Death without a break ?

I thought I should this island see
And so I sought a boatman's help;
He said the tides would raise the sea
And soon the island would be gone.

MATHEW JOSEPH

Two times a day the tides would sweep
The lonely island out of sight;
But tides would not an island keep
Submerged for long but lift themselves.

The punt-pole which the boat propelled
Dipped in water half its length;
Soon it showed a higher depth,
We felt the sea's grim, heaving strength.

A wave advanced in swirling streams
And swept across the sandy waste;
The birds now filled the air with screams
And left the submerged isle for home.

The birds come back when tides relent
And howling winds at last do cease;
Perhaps it is the land that sent
The cheering band the isle to please.

I wish some seismic force would set
The outcast island back in place.
So that the mainland would get back
Its long-lost child and be at ease.

I wish the self-same force might suck
The lagoon back to Mother Sea!
Let life's lithe waves this island sweep
And flow and swell in ebbless glee.

3.WHAT THE RIVER SAID

I clambered on to the high rock,
My body dripping with water,
And perched on its top,
Waiting for my panting breath
To quieten a little.

I planned to take another plunge
Into the brimful river,
Where I had been swimming,
My hands breast-stroking the waves
And my legs frog-kicking to reach
The other shore.
Every time I crossed the river,
I returned, climbed the rock even to its crest
And jumped down into the water again.

I jumped down as I planned.
While making my way back
To the moss-covered perch atop the rock,
I heard the river say to me in a faint whisper:
"We are alike; I do the same thing as you,
Only that I get back to my lofty perch
Atop the hill, air-borne
On the clouds' cosy back."

4.THE CARGO BOATS

Like the shadows pale afternoons bring,
The images of those cargo boats
Fall upon my mind's screen.
Slow paced and languid, they used to sail up and down
The river, laden with merchandise.
Their proud prows, brass-studded and glittering
In the sun, they moved up or down the stream,
The boatmen propelling them with their
Steel-tipped punt poles.
A long arching reedroof covered the hold.
The sliding mid-segment drawn aside for unloading,
They would berth below the bathing ghat
Two or even three abreast.
In summer, when the dry months reduced
The river to a shallow stream,
The boatmen would deepen
Their channel, drawing aside the sand,
The fine, powdery sand, gleaming with the
Presence of mica, using a plank
Which they both pushed and pulled.
Children begged to be permitted
To pull the boats upstream.
For, it was a pleasure and a privilege
For the sports-starved village kids.
They would look into the hold
Through the chinks in the boats' roof

For a glimpse of the world inside (or outside?)
The boats were no less mysterious to them
Than ships.

Gone are the boats now,
Gone indeed is the powdery sand,
Rich with the mica bits.
Gone are the children too who possessed then
Their sense of mystery.

Not the river's flood, but the flow of time
Has washed away those lovely sights.

5.UNSEEN HOSTEL MATES

The warden welcomed us and herded us
To a hall, where he spoke to us about
The rules, which he said, would keep us, of course,
If we kept them. Our morning faces fell
And assumed a dark, late after-noon look
As we listened to all those do's and don't's
That the junior students must abide by.
He led the way, we followed him behind
To what he called our home away from home.
Thus started our first day in the hostel.
Like dragon flies on Summer eves, home-thoughts
Swarmed in our minds; oh we had never thought
We loved home so much.

                          Home-sick and unquiet
I whispered messages into the air
And to the passing birds that they might tell
The people at home that I missed them all.
At the top floor the air hung heavy and
It was as if there drooped in every room,
A sapling, well-potted but still limp from
The uprooting. The hostel housed, they said,
Some eighty boys but there were more inmates,
As I was to discover soon.

At dusk
It rained, and the spouts gushed like our own minds.
As night came and shadows outgrew their shapes,
I heard a rumble coming from the loft,
A succession of shrieks and crush of wings.
A bat flung itself out, another one,
A third, a fourth, in tens, in their hundreds
The grotesque creatures came, and dipped and plunged
Into the silent night like evil stirring
In the human heart; they merged with the night.
But the night brought them back to their dark homes
Ere the sun rose; and the hordes came
Screeching their protests against the arrows keen
That had begun to fly out from the east.

Often I think of those old hostel mates,
The lawless rioters of my new home.

6.THE EVIL CHORUS

Obliged to walk across the knee-deep tide,
I floundered through the water, none too pleased;
On twigs and floating bits of wood did ride
A thousand creatures, by the flood displaced.

There sat a frog upon a stake to hail
The turbid ripples as they shoreward raced.
It sang a song of welcome but the wail
Of dying creatures drowned the raucous chant.

The fellow frogs now joined in to sing.
They splashed about and croaked exulting cries,
I felt the pain that sombre thoughts do bring
And waded on along the flooded stretch.

7.FAIRY DUST

A shaft of light fell into the attic room
Through a chink on the rusty tin roof;
Whiffs of smoke crossed the light, its diffused presence
Tinting the whole shaft.

The shaft of light showed a hidden world,
A pre-creation world, for so it seemed.
Specks of dust, millions and millions of them,
And they revealed to me how crowded
The empty attic room was.
A world that seemed to defy
The light that God let there be.
A universe in little where every planet
Seemed to look for
A sun to revolve around.

Tinted with the blue of the smoke,
The specks travelled up and down the shaft,
Fast and yet with no collisions on the way,
Disorderly and yet without disorder.
Where else but in the human mind
Does one find such crazy motion?
Every speck of dust in motion,
Every speck in suspension!
Where else but amongst the humankind
Does one find such a destiny?

8.THE WOODED STRETCH*

There, at that wooded stretch, the stream slackens
Its pace to clear its brownish, turbid flow
And to gain, besides, the bluish depths
Its purling mountain springs have never known.
Flowers drop from the pendent, spring-flushed boughs
And bedeck the stream, which flows on proudly,
Slow and graceful, grateful for what the bend
Has done to it.

                         I can't think of this stretch
That does thy northern boundary define
But my thoughts always rise to thee
O my Alma Mater! Thou hast been to us
The wooded stretch of our life's stream, for sure.
Here the currents steadied, thy stemming stress
The muddy, brownish waters got to clear.
And blessed us with the soft rhythm of depths.
As trees do drop their honeyed floral gifts
On the stream below, on my life's shy stream
There fell from thee the graces manifold.

Now, as shadows lengthen at afternoon's
Elongating pull, I am traversing
Thy sacred grounds from scenic River Front

To Main Gate.
                    Thy pastoral charm remains
Intact, for lo! the swarthy buffaloes
Dot the ground, grazing in a small herd
As in olden days. The saplings I have known
Are all trees now, their verdant, sunlit boughs
Playing mystic games with the sunshine rich.
And shadows twist and twine on the grassy ground.
The mango trees are in bloom all the way,
A herd of cars have invaded thy paths
And needs must they, for, see, the times have changed.
A bevy of girls pass by, the boys cross
My path, talking of things that please them best.

And now the great buildings burst into view;
A mighty being sure does here abide,
The grass her foot stool, silver clouds her crown.
I feel thy presence and I bow to thee.
The slanting sunlight cascades down the fronds
And streams to the ground below; I pass on
And think of the stream I was once, Mother.
                    • *A Tribute to St Thomas College, Palai*

9.THE HALLOWED GROUND

I'm standing at the hallowed place where bloomed,
As in a forcing ground, my mind and soul.
There stands my school, all smiles, my mother proud,
To welcome back her sons with feelings fond.

As when a strong blast lifts up the dead leaves
And fills the air with them and dims the view—
So do old memories criss-cross my mind
And crowd it with a host of shapes and thoughts.
My friends. my teachers. scenes of work and play.
The twang of heart-strings, laughter loud and clear,
The thrills that success brought, proud achievements,
Defeats and heartaches, the expanding mind—
All brings me back the springtime of my life.

Like to a handful of coins upwards thrown,
We left the school to fall ov'r a wide terrain;
  No coin but was picked up and treasured quite;
Gold and silver ones, we did Mother proud.

10.THE SCULPTOR AT WORK

I watched the sculptor at his work,
I saw him knead a lump of clay;
He rolled and shaped it like a globe—
A moist mass that dripping lay.

He waited till the clay was dry,
And fit to feel his fingers shake;
He knew the loamy forest hid
The lovely game he sought to take.

He pressed it down, the flattened lump
Now looked a tortoise, I should say;
A few more strokes and now it looked
A brownish fish that panting lay;

The fish form soon the man unmade
And fashioned then a quadruped;
Form followed form but pleased with none
The sculptor went on the clay to shred.

The best the lump of clay could yield—
And that too at its lovely best:
No lesser form his art would take;
The search—it progressed like a quest.

At last in flawless finish full

MATHEW JOSEPH

Emerged the human form so fine;
A smile lit up the sculptor's face;
He felt creation's thrill divine.

11.RESURRECTION

I was taking a stroll along the College Road.
The luscious, green grass lay
Basking in the morning sun,
Its tender blades listening
To the wind's lullabies.

A truck pulled up outside the wall
And workmen unloaded a pile
Of rectangular roof-sheets and set them
On the turf, one above the other.

To me, the pile looked like a tomb
And the thought of the life-brimming grass
Which was to die, so that an old building
May have a new roof haunted my mind.

It rained in the night and with dirt
Rainwater scored an epitaph on the tomb,
The usual thing about everything being dust.

The pile stood in its place for six months.
To the grass beneath, the pile was like winter,
But when winter ends,
Spring brings the herbage back to life;
  The grass the pile has interred
Was gone for good, I thought.

One day the pile was lifted leaving
A rectangular patch, which showed
The markings of lizards and centipedes
But no trace of any grass;

It rained that night,
The peal of thunder rolling
Endlessly; as if in response to the peal,
The bladeless roots stirred
And in about a week's time
The barren rectangular patch was dotted
With buds of green.
As I passed by
A month later, the luscious, green blades
Were listening to the wind's lullabies.

12.THE LONE SURVIVOR

Dripping with darkness on the teak-tree boughs,
Like grotesque fruits hanging from some weird tree,
And upside down the ugly fox-bats lay.
Their nocturnal forays that took them down
The slow veins and arteries of the night
Had ended with the night's end, unscratched
Even by a fire-fly's light. Another day
To rest or screech or crawl up the boughs
Or gaze at the earth below or wait
For the sun to set and bring the night on—
Night is the board on which the bats feasted,
The Horn of plenty, the fruits cascading
Down its dark brim in endless plenitude.
The quince, the peach, the plantain, mangos, plum,
The   ripe areca, cycus, jack fruits too.
Their earth gazing eyes watched the shadows twist
And turn down there and their dim eyes did see
Their own shadows marking the ground below.

A man with a fowling piece took aim, a shot
Rang out. A flutter of leathern wings, a cloud
Of screeching bats rose in the air, aghast.

MATHEW JOSEPH

The one the bullet hit hung dead on the bough
Too tight its grip to let the body fall.
Its shadow fell close to the hunter, though.

23

13.AN EDEN THAT IS EVIL: A SESTINA

If they're looking for fruits, those hungry birds
Will find them near at hand, for by that stream
There's an orchard where fruit trees dot the ground
In such abundance that e'en the bright sun
Can scarce find a way through the verdant growth
To kiss the grass that loves its warmth and light.

The birds have found the trees; their foot-falls light
Sway the lithe boughs that bear the hungry birds.
Their wings half spread, searching among the growth
Of shrubs and plants and trees the purling stream
Has nurtured with its life and with the sun
To help, the birds sit a man's height from the ground.

I watch all birds in the sky or on the ground
And so shading my eyes against the light,
I see those birds, their bright feathers in the sun,
The colourful fruits they eat, the games the birds
Play teetering on the boughs, the rich stream
And all the movements in the undergrowth.

How fast this orchard grew! Its fecund growth
Is due, no doubt, to the fertile ground;

The trees should thank besides the silver stream
That downwards drives the roots, and boughs to light.
From far and wide the orchard draws the birds
That twitter, feed and play, screened off from the sun.

I see a darksome cloud approach the sun,
I hear a flutter in the undergrowth;
Loud screeches rend the air, the feasting birds—
They watch a tragic scene now on the ground.
A snake has caught a fledgling and the light,
It fades; the birds leave Eden and the stream.

Across the dale, unconcerned flows the stream,
'Life feeds on life' the orchard knows; the sun
Now bright again, floods the tree-tops with light
And lets its searching beams seep through the growth
And makes a stream of light across the ground.
My scanning eyes pursue the flight of birds.

It is the stream that gave the orchard growth
Or is it the sun or the fertile ground?
An Eden of light, it meant evil to the birds.

14.THE TERMITE MOUNDS

The termite mounds that dot that wooded field
Are each a wonder—Nature's proud design.
I think they're coeval with the trees out there--
The teak, the jungle jack, the lovely pine.

Inside the mound a maze of pathways leads
To cells or chambers, small or large in size;
A royal couple rules the termite land
With workers blind that help the brood to raise.

A princely class of winged termites they raise
And when the nest with wingers gets to teem,
Great Nature drops the signal, all at once
Their bridal flight they start and skywards stream.

The gnomes thus become sylves, the princely class—
They flounder up on their tenuous wings:
A living fountain from the earth's entrails--
An upward flowing stream that hums and sings.

But life on life does feed, so on the way
The living fountain thins and soon is lost;
A host of birds and bats in circles fly
Eating up the flies at little cost.

A fly or two survive, the bridal pair

Descend and back to darksome earth repair;
In course of time there sprouts another mound
And sets the stage for another bridal fair.

When those trees were young and I a little child
We used to bet which bird shall catch which fly;
The show still continues with fewer birds
But children choose to miss the show so nigh.

15. POOR PAUL

I heard a conversation from the room
And waited at the door for manners' sake;
The door was closed but two voices I heard,
They talked and talked like people half awake.

They talked and talked—both seemed a little cracked.
One called the other names, a litany
Of names followed and then they sued for peace.
Again they clashed, again they called a truce.

Then I heard the one to the other say:
"No wonder, lousy Raphael cut your throat."
Great God! A ghostly tryst? My body quaked;
My spirit, nonetheless, the fears fought.

A spell of silence; then, the door opened.
A haggard figure came out followed by none.
Later that day when I this story told,
A neighbour said, "That's Paul, the crazy one."

"Paul talks to himself—in a sense, I mean.
Paul simulates his brother's voice, make-believes
That from death's other kingdom Michael's come
And talks and talks till the other one leaves.

"His brother's murder—it left his brain deranged,
Despite the fights, each loved the other well.

MATHEW JOSEPH

Their quarrels were a way of showing love;
Paul vows he'll revenge have though he lands in hell."

16.THE EUPHORIC BUDDHA

I often think of Raj, the town drunkard,
Who wore, when drunk, a beatific face.
He claimed to be the Buddha, Wisdom's crown,
And sought to enlighten the sober guys.

Emboldened by the bottle, one with Truth,
He walked along the streets and cast the pearls—
The pearls of wisdom fell before the 'swine'
Who knew the Buddha's brain was full of snarls.

He urged all men to get rid of desires,
And march along the path of peace to bliss;
He spiced his speeches with learned words,
So might the listeners ne'er its meaning miss.

But it ne'er got into the listeners' hearts;
Of bad repressions and complexes born,
His discourse lacked the depth of simple truth
But showed a stupid mind, by longings torn.

.

One day a fellow drunk hit him on the head,
To know the contents—a search for truth's sake!
The Buddha died; the drunk was promptly nabbed;
He said he thought the head would never break.

17.A CANINE FRIEND

I just asked the stray dog its name,
Its tail wagged in reply;
I called him Wag and thus did start
A friendship on the sly.

I let him steal a thing or two
And did not shout or shoo;
He had a special wag for me,
He wagged his hind legs too.

When monsoon lashed the hapless beast,
I let him have a nest;
The dog I kept, the rightful one,
Loved him under protest.

The mornings saw him roam the town,
At noon he took a nap;
And then he'd call at friendly homes
And play the decent chap.

He came to me for lunch or snacks,
More a guest than beggar;
He'd keep away, If I was with friends
If alone, he'd swagger.

He fights his battles on the way,
Barks and snarls and growls;
How else can Wag remain alive,

When Death to catch him prowls?

A brindled dog of modest size,
Agile and strong he is;
The world is wide, our hearts are large,
God! Let his tribe increase.

18.THE LIBERATOR

A hot and sultry day it was,
A day in mid-July.
The treeless plain, all wrapped in dust,
Half dead in the sun did lie.

Eager to slake her parching thirst,
For clouds she scanned the sky;
None seemed to come in the bluish waste
To lose itself and die.

The dusty roads—a sorry sight—
Criss-crossed the plain, like bands;
I thought of someone on a stake,
Sprawled out with outstretched hands.

The hapless victim writhed in pain,
To feel the scorching torch;
A thousand flames of horrid heat,
The whole landscape did parch.

An object like a human fist,
Was seen to cross the sky.
It grew in size, it was a cloud,
It hung above on high.

Like swords the lightnings flashed above,
To cut the bands, it seemed;

The heavy downpour doused the torch,
A grateful plain—she beamed.

19. THE MONSOON CLOUDS

They race across the sky—the monsoon clouds.
God's plenty of shapes. Specks and bars
And sheets with long irregular rents.
Piled up masses, curls and tenuous bits.
All straggling towards the zenith, lumbering yet forceful.
Their motion and the gray uniform they flaunt
Betoken some mission, dark or white.

How different they are from the colourful clouds
That herald the sun's arrival! Or from those
That decorate the western gate
Through which the sun exits!
Or from the lazy cumulous clouds
That trail their slow shadows
Across the sun-drenched plain,
Each minute a different shape!
Or from the lone rain cloud around whose rim
The argent sunshine cascades!

20.THE PHOSPHORESCENT GLOW

A team of workers were digging a piece
Of fallow farm-land, bringing their spades down
In unison to the simple rhythm
Of an old folk song.
In a wide circle they stood
And the loose, turned up lumps of soil
Rose in the air,
Dancing to the same song.

The land was being laid for paddy crop.
The choric song—it sang about the man
Who hid his gold in the earth and lost the gold
To the earth.
For years the land had fallow lain;
The spades now sought to clear the weedy ground
And wrest this field from Nature's mighty hands.
The circle narrowed,
Cries of joy rang out from the workers' throat;
 The dug-up field was now fit for seeds.

That night I chanced to walk along the path
Which edged the turned up field and lo!—

MATHEW JOSEPH

A sight to see it was!
The broken lumps all glowed
With an eerie yellow light and the dark background
Glimmered in the glow; surprised I exclaimed:
"Who has sown this field with seeds of light?"
The seeds that had sprouted were the phosphorus
That had lain in the earth, for long years,
Hoarded by the earth; the phosphorescence,
The sight of the clods glowing in the field,
The spendthrift exuberance of the soil,
It still haunts my mind, despite Time's passage.

21.FIRE ON THE HILL

The distant hill from which this river springs
Goes dry in summer once the rains do end;
The grass which clothes the craggy hill in green
Would then grow shabby, dry and downward bend.

A stone, dislodged and sliding down the hill,
May strike a boulder standing in its path;
The crash would light a fire and burn the grass,
The flames advancing like reapers at the swath.

The slops would then lie parching in the sun
And night winds whirl or waltz or trip about;
When lovely April comes with mist and rain,
From ashes springs the phoenix, wings spread out.

With eager eyes I used to watch the fire
Engulf the slops with golden ripples bright;
The shallow summer stream the show imaged,
And water seemed to burn with yellow light.

The water that my feet does gently stroke
Has stroked the luscious grass that drapes the hill.
The fire that cleaned the slops and brought new life
Is burning in my thoughts and memory still.

22.THE DEAD SEA

A short car-ride from Qumran took us past
The arid plains to where its deadness crowns
The landscape with a lake where nothing lives.
The bare terrain dipped—to underworld
It seemed—and sun-drenched before us we saw
The great Trough from which the Centuries
Have slaked their thirst, leaving the denser dregs
Untouched; though dead, not deadly, for it lets
The tourists lie afloat on its bosom;
Not dead either; the swimmers splashed and dived
Like shoals of fish and their shadows moved below
Like greyish water plants; and it lapped up
The trickles which the river Jordan brought
And breathed and heaved its bosom like one in sleep.
The lake may not know, here the Great Glacier
Dug its heels into the earth, eons ago
While being pulled south by Nature's rifting force.

23. THE OLD CHURCH

Atop the hill there stands the church
Our great grand-fathers built;
It guards their bones and sadly views
The town their children built.

Sun-lit upon the river bank
A stately city stands;
A boom-town with a quickened pulse
And high-tensed arteries.

Six days a week our fathers strove
To further expand it;
Sundays a few went up the hill,
To pray, the rest idled.

We found that Church too high to reach
And built the lower one;
Half-hid among the market blocks
And lone, the New Church stands.

We left the hill-top one to bats;
Now as the sun goes down,
In screeching tones they thank the Lord
That dark is come again.

The case that held the vigil lamp

Is dark, the font is dry
Except when the broken tiles
Let in God's wind and rain.

Our children may not see the church
Our great grand-fathers built.
Or will they? There's no telling sure
When some structures fall.

24.UNWORTHY FOREHEADS

He's on his way to church; his car speeds fast
Along the dusty road, pursued by Dust,
The rear glass framing the relentless chase.

Dust pursues whatever moves along this way
And imprints its brown seal to signify,
So it seems, its terrible masterhood.

It's summer at its height and no green clings
To the withered grass-blades or to the shrubs,
Brown with their coat of dust; a peal of bells
Is heard; the church is reached, the front glass frames
The hill-top church with the tall spire and cross
Behind which hides a lightning arrester.

It is Ash Wednesday; at church he kneels
As the priest walks down the aisle imprinting
The cross on each forehead with charcoal paste
Whose glossy black outshines the brown of Dust.
A smudge of black he gets: the church is filled
With crosses of all kinds, a well formed cross
Is a rarity though. The mass begins;
Throughout the mass he notes the incense smoke
Eddy under the fans that block its way.
The homeward trip; a cloud of dust pursues
The car that speeds away: the rear glass shows
The Dust and through it a distant spire cross.

25. A GAME

Some way out on the moon-lit lake,
Afloat and drifting with the wind,
A bloated carcass lay, its wake
Alive with swarms of feasting fish.

A splash! Another splash! A third!
The ripples raced in panic; splash!
A man was pelting stones; I heard
An exulting cry, a loud laugh.

I had come out to watch the waves
Gather gold from rich moon-light's ore;
To hear the wind's song as it heaves
The slanting willows on the shore.

The fireflies barred with golden thread
My path; I walked on; in the skies
The shooting stars did featly tread
A cosmic dance to lure my eyes.

And then it was I heard the splash
And saw the fly-blown carcass float.
Each time he hit the bloated mash
He yelled and laughed in wild delight.

Foul wind flourished its sword of stench;
I fled—the crazy man may boast
He played the game he played and won
Full splashy scores at little cost.

26. FELINE MUSIC

Rosy, my cat, is purring;
The satisfied cry my cat makes
When patted on her gray coat and limbs
Is sweeter to me
Than all the sweetness
That sweet sounds keep in them
Like nectar in the flower buds;
It's a cry of contentment,
An utterance meaning love,
An open acknowledgement
That life's good;
It is my dearest of dear sounds:
She seems to respond to my stroking hands
Modulating the purrs to my fingers' touch.
Now dull, now loud, always heard, like the hum
Of a well-oiled machine it rolls on,
A hymn in praise of serene contentment.

How different the sound is from the insistent
Miaows with which she demands her food
Or from the dull mews she lets out,
Tail upright and brushing against my legs with her head,
Or from the warning cries
With which she keeps her kitten from wandering!

27.A BOYHOOD EXPERIENCE

Before I reached the beach, the sun had dipped,
The gloaming gloomed the sky, the billows sobbed;
My first encounter with the sea it was,
My heart, in vain, for the Mighty Being throbbed.

Too late I was to see the sea but yet
I heard its moan and touched and felt the brine;
To rest at night we sought a lodging house
Though little thought I I had to rest or dine.

Throughout the night I heard the dash of waves,
Throughout the night it kept me wide awake;
All night the howling winds did prowl around;
I felt uneasy and my mind did quake.

But when it dawned, I saw a different scene,
A gold and silver scene, a scene so bright:
I saw the sea, a work of art, it looked.
God's splendid poem writ for man's delight.

The rhythmic beat, the magic and the charm,
The depth, the beauty—all this there combined;
It stunned me with a shock too huge for words,

It still with wonder all my thoughts does bind.

46

28.THE BRIGADES OF THE NIGHT

I cupped my hands around the fragile flame,
  Kept it going despite the winds outside.
The wind, it seemed, was out to kill the light,
And bring its friends, the lawless hordes, inside.

Blast after blast I helped the flame survive;
A lull there came; the winds slackened a bit;
Again the storm picked up, the slanting rain
Pelting on the panes as though the glass to slit.

The droplets glistened in the yellow glow
And slid down the glass in a stream of light.
Fixed in the sconce the burning candle stood,
A fighter lone that darkness did affright.

But darkness has its ways dark ends to gain;
A beetle dark in night's livery dressed
Hurled itself on the flame and out it went;
The fight I fought was lost, I felt depressed.

29."INLAND FAR THOUGH WE BE"

I clambered up the rock atop the hill
And looked towards the west to try and see
The dim-seen blue beyond the crimson clouds—
The glimmer faint of the distant, bluish sea.

There hung the sun above the western marge,
And viewed through the thin clouds the restless sea;
Full forty miles inland I stood and watched
Eager to see the scene the sun did see.

Rare indeed are the moments when the sea
Yields to searching eyes and lifts the veil;
With shaded eyes the sun-set sky I scanned,
Where clouds in layers lay to drift or sail.

Then through a sudden gap the sea I saw —
The sea, the sea, the bluish band I sought!
I clambered down the rock with delight dazed,
A descent from the skies with pleasure fraught.

The vision blessed the seeker hopes to find
And questing spends his days, by hope sustained;
Then comes the golden day that lifts the veils
And shows the throne of Truth, all pure unstained

30. GOD'S NAMESAKE

It seemed that God did not care for his namesake.
How else could Ishwar fail all the six parts
He played to make a bare living--to keep
The wolf from the door ? He farmed, he tailored,
He ran errands, cooked, sold peanuts on the streets,
And kept the bees, on borrowed capital.
Bee-keeping he quit when he discovered
Their true nature; One day, stung all over
By the angry swarm, he burned the hives down.
He blamed the bees for it, for he found the bees
Not sweetness and light, but stings and stickiness.
But he always thought that good days were ahead
And pledged his future wealth for present loans.
Now, as I think about him, the hoary mist
Of oblivion parts and I see the man
Walk into my neighbour's house for a loan
Of this kind. He says he will pledge a chair
Which, his Namesake willing, he might get
From a donor whose name he won't reveal.
Ishwar got all the money he hoped to get,
For, his desperate effort not to beg,
Rather than the chair, impressed the lender.

31.MOSES—A MONOLOGUE

Tell me to what place this dusty way leads.
Does it go to the great hill from whose crest
I can see the Promised Land of my dreams?
I tried for a glimpse of it from there once
But mists obscured my view; I saw only
Hoary haze wilfully veiling the vale.

Do you say you do not know? But this place
Is your home ground, you old mountain shepherd.
My people are waiting out there, eager,
Impatient, anxious and dying for a glimpse.
The Lord, I should say, is not wholly pleased
With me; your face tells me you want to know
What displeased the Lord. Those clouds sailing there
Look like the boats on the Nile, with sails out,
The papyrus boats that make their way upstream
Brushing the bulrushes on the low banks.

A hard time we've had crossing the deserts
And afflicted with dire thirst, my people cried
For water, said it was my fault they had
No water to drink; you never feel thirst
In the Land the Lord promised. It flows with
Honey and milk but that's a distant dream.

They'd rather be Pharaoh's slaves than endure
A parching throat, freedom or no freedom.

The Lord had pity on me; "Speak Moses
Thou to the rock and it will yield to thee
The water it has hoarded under it,"
The Lord said, but rather than speak to it,
I struck the rock; the staff persuades better
Than words; I spare all words, for the rod is surer
To yield results; the Red Sea did divide
When I stretched out my hand with the rod in it.
What good is your sheepcrook if not to catch
The errant sheep? But the Lord was displeased
That I disobeyed him. Had not he led us
Through the deserts' waste and showed us our way
Night and day, with pillars of fire and smoke?
I am sorry; beyond that mountain ridge
Hides the Promised Land I will never see.
You shepherd, take thy flocks to the pasture
And let the flocks drink from the still waters
And graze on the green grass—my starving flocks
The human flocks that follow me in hope,
I will not lead them…Lord I am sorry.

32.THE MAN WITH THE SICKLE

We were at play in a lovely garden.
A hoary headed man with a sickle
Asked us, children, to leave the garden ground
And take the upland trail to where it led.
Up there we'd find vacant lots to play in.

To leave those happy grounds! It sounded like death.
We had romped around along its pathways
Chasing butterflies, had played and frolicked
In the arbours there, had outstripped the clouds
And made friends with trees to which we gave
What names it pleased us to call them; we swarmed
Around the fruit-trees looking for windfalls;
None barred our way, the owner having gone
To the hills where he lived close to the sky.

We demurred but the man with the sickle—
He brooked no protests; we heard the tall gate
Close behind us. The way the man watched us!
His sickle ov'r his eyes, the man still watched
The sad evictees moving up the hill.

33. LIFE IS A GAME OF CHANCE

He ran a small grocery store,
He opened it for fun;
He chose a forlorn nook for fear
Else he'd have leisure none.

He sought no pleasure profits brought
He loved the game of whist.
The shop was just a place to play
The game that none resist.

His whole effort would centre on
A foursome how to cast.
The game begun, the buyers got
A 'no-stock' sign, at best.

As customers did come and go,
He said like one aggrieved:
"Shops galore that sell such things."
His guests—they all agreed.

Be it salt or rice or sugar
The grocer said "No stock".
But what was there in stock for him
Was Fate's unseemly joke.

The craze for whist got worse and soon

His life in ruin lay.
He took to peddling in the streets
And house to house did stray.

34.OLD SIMON

He told us stories of the fox and crane,
Of dwarfs, of princes and of warlocks bold.
The piper pied whose flute the children charmed
Could learn more potent charms from Simon old.

He stayed with us and dug the farm for us;
His room, a lean-to with a bedstead old.
For bed-time stories we besieged him there
And watched in wonder the fable-world unfold.

The stories came from Grimm, from Anderson,
They came from Aesop and the eastern world.
We wondered how a man like Simon could,
Such vast and varied wealth in stories hold.

What fortune's wreck had brought him there none knew,
Or why he chose this place or whence had come;
His past lay buried in a tomb elsewhere--
A living ghost he was and he kept mum.

One night he indulged our wish to hear of Lear
But Simon, who could narrate tragic fate
With scarce a tremor in his manly voice,
Broke down midway and excused it was late.

35. THE COFFEE TREES IN BLOOM

The coffee trees are in bloom everywhere,
The gentle wind wafts the fragrance abroad;
The humming honey-bees the trees do swarm;
How sweet and serene looks the valley broad!

Like tufts of snow that fell during the night,
The blossoms white do cling to coffee trees;
What magic got the trees to bloom like this?
What wand the stalks did charm to draw the bees?

It is the rain that fell a week ago,
The rain that brought the parching earth solace.
It bathed the trees and seeping to the ground
It got the roots to weave a robe of grace.

A day or two –the whiteness will be brown.
A ring of green berries their place will take;
From green to yellow and to red they'll grow
Then summer rains will bring the call to wake.

36.PROSPECTORS

When in the east rich gold was struck,
We hailed the news with shouts of joy;
Our hearts aglow with dreams of gold,
Set out we soon—a large convoy.

We crossed the plains and climbed the hills,
Endured the chill of autumn eves;
The sombre sun was losing heat,
He eyed us through the falling leaves.

Yet on we climbed the bold ascents,
The way was hard, it hurt the feet.
The stunted trees, all gaunt and gnarled—
They seemed to warn of snows and sleet.

Oppressed by surly winds and snows
We pulled up—some did protest though;
There lay below, the place we sought,
A rocky valley, deep in snow.

The place we stopped at was a town,
A little town of friendly folk;
They said the valley held no gold,
And quipped our search was just a joke.

They said they too had come from far,
To prospect but had found no gold;
They chose to make the hill their home,

And learnt to face the winds so cold.

We too could do the same, they said,
And make the hill-town home with them;
We chose, a few did rebel though,
To end the quest for gold or gem.

The ones who rebelled reached the plain,
Despite the cold winds' eerie screams;
They saw the glitter on Death's teeth,
And sank to rest with gold-less dreams.

We feel the lure of gold no more,
We hoard no wealth to fill Death's pit;
To be alive is wealth enough,
Why fritter life to secure it?

It took a journey to the east
To rid us of the lust for gold;
We feel much richer for the change,
The gold we got is the wisdom old.

37.A STROLL IN THE TOWN

The sun was sliding down the western slope;
A mass of clouds, some grey, some purple or red
  Lay spread across the sky, the lazy winds
Darning their ragged edges with a clumsy hand.

Along the city road I strolled, and watched
The urban scenes-- the casual scenes of life.
A troop of merry children romped about
In the streets, their little hearts brimful of joy.
I saw a man looking among the plants
For a coin he had lost; on the park bench
A youth was lost in reading newspapers.
A street play was on at the Temple Square;
A beggar on crutches stopped by and watched
The play and laughed and laughed till he felt choked.
I walked past a row of hawkers selling
Their wares to where a snake charmer performed
Before a knot of people; a drunkard
Crawled along the road on all fours; mothers
Waited at the stops for school buses
To take their children home;
                                                    Now, many more
Scenes come to the mind as I recollect.

But the two scenes that stand out like golden threads
In my memory's web are the children
And the beggar whose rollicking laughter
Sounded like a bell celebrating life.
They alone could laugh in a busy crowd.
.

The slow, sombre clouds moved on to the west,
Light falling through two rents; I watched.

38.TRAPPED
ASHORE

A torch was flung from East's high hills,
It blazed across the sky
And fell at last in West's wide deeps
And went out all at once.

The torch was gone too soon for me
To find my port and ship;
Wave after wave of molten dark
Now drove me far inland:

So far that when the stars glistened
I saw no sea nor ship;
Then I saw a glint, a glow
On East's high hills again.

A torch came blazing once again,
And tides of darkness ebbed;
I chased the ebbing waves of gloom
In hope the sea to reach;

But no such luck! It gloomed again
Before the sea I reached.
It seemed the torch did light my path
To darker spells of gloom.

My hapless plight to shuttle on
Between the day and night!
Whoever flings the torch up there
Might laugh to see me here.

39.TWO RIVERS

Holding on to the rails of the view-point,
I took a god's eye view of the landscape
That lay below. A magnificent sight!
A thousand things for the eye to feast on.
Huge clouds lumbered ov'r the plain, their shadows
Seeking to tether them to some safe peg.
A river meandered through the woods and meads,
Its waters sparkling in the lovely sun.
The river—it imaged the silver clouds
And bound for opposite destinations
They hastened -- each to become the other.

There flowed another 'river' close to it,
But higher, a system of conveyor belts
That screeched and clanged its weary way uphill
Carrying iron ore to some plant somewhere.
I watched it till it went past the domed church
And its yard with the yew-trees lining it.
An elevated highway it appeared--
One that drove itself—to some hilly site.
To me it looked a counter flow, like life,
To the dead flux of things. Laden with iron ore,
It moved uphill, eager to reach the plant
Where those grey lumps will be crushed and processed
For their metal. The dross will go back

To the dry earth. The rails my fingers clutched
Could have ridden these belts to reach this place.
Are we not ourselves lumps on some belts?
The clouds drifted on, trailing their shadows.
I took my eyes away from the landscape;
No more a god, I moved to lower ground.

40.THE FLOW-
TIDE OF LIFE

The river was in spate, the surging currents
Leaped over the banks, the billows wild
Rushing past the trees
And forcing the little creatures of the earth
To swarm up the tree-trunks.

All kinds of debris came floating by
In the brownish water
From entire tree trunks to bud-shields and coconut husks.
The middle of the field where I stood knee-deep
In water--a little knoll--showed above the water,
A Noah's Ark of assorted creatures
Waiting for some Ararat.

Flushed out by the flood the little creatures came
Swimming towards the knoll to take refuge
There in that last bastion that held out:
Lizards and rodents, scorpions, bugs, beetles , worms—
What could they do against the torrent that roared
But stick together and wait and that they did.

The surly waters splashed around this isle of life
And would have swept across it
But the waves felt a weakness, a pull from behind.
The flood had started to fall.

As the waters ebbed and withdrew to the river course
Life's flow-tide rippled down the knoll
And swept across the field.

41. A MORNING RIDE

I rowed the boat across the river wide,
One sunny morning just to please a whim;
The ripples raced in circles as my ride
Advanced into the placid waters dim.
The river flowed, the fishes swam upstream,
The clouds were seen to drift across the sky;
The swallows chirped, the gulls and cranes did scream,
The fishers dived, the eagles watched on high.
The clouds their shadows upon the water trailed,
The winds in gentle draughts the willows heaved;
Towards the shore along a curve I sailed
Then turned around and back to shore I moved.

The ride was worth the while, I felt refreshed,
The scenes, so full of motion, got me braced.

42.THE PILGRIM'S PROGRESS

When autumn brings the bloom to mango trees,
And slims the streams and makes their music thin,
When crofts and fields await the hill-born breeze
And mornings preen their foggy bodies clean:
The cries of pilgrims ring out in the air,
Who trek uphill to cleanse their souls of sin;
Along the hilly tracts their feet do fare,
To lift themselves to God, his grace to win.
Brimful of faith their hearts and set on God,
Their minds a lyre, vibrating with pious thought.
With ardent steps the upward trail they plod,
Their souls full worthy of the grace they sought.

A longer version of this quest is life,
An arduous climb through perils, pain and strife.

43. A SHIP IN THE SKY

I thought I saw a ship atop a hill,
I saw it list and right itself again;
It moved ahead to ride a storm in vain
And lumbered on the winds but risked to sail;
No ship, for sure, can get atop a hill,
Unless some flood arose and helped it gain
The dizzy heights, the clouds' serene domain
Like the Deluge that heaved the Ark uphill.

The ship I saw was ship only in shape;
A cloud it was, a multi-layered cloud;
But like a ship it took me lands away,
To far off climes to which it let me 'scape.
It made me think of Noah and the crowd
Of beasts , of Ararat and the Flood's sway.

44. A MORNING WALK

I sauntered through the streets at break of day,
A pleasant day it promised, warm and bright;
A lucent morn it was in flowery May
When Nature's at her lovely glories' height.

A golden mood now did my mind possess:
The road ahead, it seemed a carpet red;
I felt if on along the way I pressed,
My feet would heaven's hallowed precincts tread.

The world, I thought, was of Goodness formed,
And flawless was the plan the world did guide;
Up in the air a light-winged kestrel roamed
Like my own soul which then in glee did glide.

A beggar crossed my path, the rags he wore
Fluttered in mockery of the morning's glows:
Then came a feeble man with sightless eyes
Warding off a dog with blundering blows.

My buoyant mood—it took a dip, the road
No longer had the carpet red it wore—
The kestrel soaring up to heaven's gate
Locked in a fight, fell , its downs splotched with gore.

45.THE ROAD TO THE CLOUDS

Where does that road go, twining up the hills,
As does a vine around a jungle tree?
It looks like a stream climbing up the hill,
With waterfalls in reverse, forced upstream
By some strange inversion of the earth's pull.
Wet with the dews, the road glistens in the sun,
Each dew a marvel with the sun inside.
A road to God's presence, beyond the clouds!
For so it looks; but the truth, I know,
Is what the bearded man whispered to me;
He said the road goes to the coastal town
Where the land ends and an uncharted sea
Lashes against the land like mad, daunting
The sailors.

       And this man told me further:
"Up there when you get, the sun will sure have paved
The road with sheets of gold. So high you go
The clouds --they brush you by and trailing them behind
You wend your way. The kestrels greet the day,
The new-born day, which, as it brightens up,
Would reveal new-sown fields of wheat below.
And many brooks not far from their sources.
You cast a long shadow on the ground,

So big, you look an infant in its arms.
With gay abandon you trip on and on
Till the long shadow hides under your feet."
.

Midway the path begins to dip, he said,
Towards a pleasant plain of scenic charm.
A plain of bright sunshine and fiery flowers,
Of fields and groves on whose verdant trees
The song-birds weave a web of melody.
And purling brooks the lovely landscapes cross,
Whose crystal waters hug the silver sands.

Then would I come, he said, to soggy ground,
A gloomy landscape would the traveller see;
A stretch of stunted trees and stumps and sloughs.
A wilderness of shapes, as dazed as sleep's,
Against a dreary afternoon of gloom.
My shadow, now at large, would grow in size
And trip me up from behind as daylight wanes.
With night-fall will the journey end, the winds
Muffling all sounds save the dash of waves.

"You should not quail or falter," said the man
"When to the pleasant plain your back is turned —
When slanting light of gloomy afternoon
Cascades like a stream down the yellow leaves—
When shadows teem around you like the scouts
Of some Dark Power citadelled not far off—
Or when the empty fields and lonely trees
 Their sombre plight in hoary mist conceal.
Spend a restful night when the town is reached
And wait for the passage across the sea."
Whence this intelligence—I do not know.
Or who the man that spoke to me these words.

MATHEW JOSEPH

The staff he leaned on looked a question mark.
Its shadow on the ground another mark.

46.THE WELCOME ARCH

From the south-western corner of the sky,
The clouds emerged like sheep out of their folds
And raced across the aerial plains to play
And graze and gambol on the eastern hills.
The darkness they were locked in had bedaubed
Their fleece, the dark grey of which no sunlight
Could soften or subdue; a zone of light
The east looked in contrast to the dark west.
The winds were seen to herd the straggling clouds
And fuse and weld them to a mass that moved.

Who has ever heard of arrows   shooting
A bow? But oh I saw it happen there.
The sun's gold-tipped rays, each hiding a riot
Of colours sped across the sky towards
The moving mass of clouds and fixed on it
A splendid rainbow, bright and wonderful.
There stood this arch of beauty glowing bright
Between whose violet rim and reddish hem
Mine eyes perceived the inside of heaven.
A drizzle fell   brightening the rainbow,
The spectrum glowing clearer, band by band.

MATHEW JOSEPH

A welcome arch the bow looked, bestriding
The land for whose liberation from drought
The clouds had come, the bow the sun's assurance
That the deluge of dust will sure subside.

47.THE BENEFACTOR

They came, their tails wagging with excitement,
In ones and twos, eager to be in time
For lunch, the impossible dream come true.
A score or more—the sentries of the streets.
They sat at the road bay, their heads all turned
Towards the College Road and their ears pricked
To catch the drone of the yellow vehicle
That brought their lunch with their benefactor
Behind the wheel. The very thought of him—
The tall cassocked man who loved the dogs,
The friend of all the creatures great and small—
Set their tails wagging.
                          The car pulled up
Beside the bay. A chorus of loud howls
Rose from their throats, a chorus of yells and moans,
Of half suppressed barks and loud friendly growls.
A scramble seemed imminent but the priest
His arms akimbo, called for silence strict,
And spoke to them; meanwhile his assistant,
Who had no mind to spare the rod,
Set down their lunch and fed the hungry lot.
An Oliver Twist or two asked for more,
A demand they did not press. Now; to stray—
Their duty—they dispersed, a few remained.

MATHEW JOSEPH

The yellow car, its wheels, in three places wet,
Moved past the stragglers' wagging tails and left.

48.THE ONE WHO SPREAD LIGHT

Little Johnny Thin's mission, I guess,
Was to illumine all interiors.
He stood in the courtyard
With a mirror in his hands,
The up-end of which he held
Touching his chest and the lower one
In his hand at the appropriate angle.
He let the sun explore every room of his house
Though it meant, for the sun,
Climbing through the windows.
He then trained the light
On his people in the living room;
An educative experience it was,
For it proved that people
Dislike light. It was angry shouts,
Not appreciative words, that he got.
Though he did not know it, he was
In good company;
All purveyors of light
Have shared the same fate.
A man came out of the room
Swishing a came

MATHEW JOSEPH

And the live periscope fled.

79

49.A DAY IN JUNE

The day dawned with far less glory, the winds
Invading the sky with rank on rank of clouds;
A faint glimmering round was all that was seen
Of the sun who would otherwise blaze the sky
With golden light and shred all the shades
And make them crawl along the ground; it rained
For ov'r an hour, the muddy water gushed
In torrents strong and filled and flooded quite
All the open lots where sunlight would else
Have lain in pools; when the rain let up, shafts
Of sunshine fell from the sky through the gaps
The boughs made and gifted rainbows to the drops
Of water dangling on the edge of leaves.
It rained again as it should in wet June,
Blustering winds ushering in the storm.
At last a lull did come and through the thin clouds
Soft sunlight seeped in like the sun's own smile.
The smile broadened into a riot of light,
And shadows crawled along the ground again
But wouldn't let go their hold—the realms they held.
Clouds massed in the sky again, the sun
By now had reached the sky's descending slope.
There sat an aged man by the wayside
Watching the changing day and in what he saw

MATHEW JOSEPH

He might well have seen his own life unreeling.

81

50.TWO QUESTERS*

They were born, for great things were to happen.
Halley's resplendent comet swept across
The sky, training its flaming trail, torch-like,
At the sleeping earth, as if to decide
Where the two wonders of abounding grace
That great God was pleased to bless the world with
Were to be born; in Macedonia's
Distant north Agnes was born, in India's
Palm-studded south Anna. Each not aware
Of the other, they yearned for the great Lord
Of the skies and chose him as their heart's Lord.
The winds spoke to them of him, the mountains
Confirmed the winds' words, the bejewelled skies—
They spoke to them of loveliness that lasts.

Thus started their quest for the Lord Divine.
The world showed them the 'primrose path' and urged
Them to take it; for it led through the woods
To life's splendid carnival; but averse
To any shape but the Lord's, they wended
Their different ways uphill, each on her side
Of the mountain. The journey took longer
For Agnes, for she stopped for every one
Who needed help; the lowly and the lost,
The sick, the destitute, the orphans, slaves,

The men with parching minds, the spring of hope
Having gone dry; she felt she sure did see
In those unlucky faces the Lord's face
In disguise; the trail lay in bold ascent
And mid-way she took a surer trail;
The new one seemed to give a better view
Of the house up-hill; with unfaltering steps
She moved and got at last to the Lord's gates.

As for Anna, the way was hard, it hurt
Her tender feet; the brambles barred her way;
The travellers she fell in with advised
That she might return to the 'primrose path'
And fare in comfort; Some called her a fake;

She trudged along, despite all the trials,
Despite the cloudy weather and the fogs.
Then like a pack of wolves illnesses came;
The worst affliction was those spells of storm
When darksome clouds covered the hill-top home
And filled the lonely heart with sore distress.
She trudged on falling and picking herself up
To fall again. She did not need to climb
All the way up but half way up the hill
The Lord himself came in triumph to her.

The questers met at last on the rampart
Of God's house and from there they watched this earth
Of ours that "spins like a fretful midge".

*A tribute to St Alphonsa and Mother Theresa, on the occasion
of their 100th birth day.*